THE OPEN ROAD

THE OPEN ROAD

WALT WHITMAN
ON DEATH & DYING

Edited by Joe Vest

To the Reader

You may notice that this book lacks certain features usually
found in such a volume such as table of contents, numbered pages,
footnotes and an index. We have consciously omitted these features
because of the special meditative nature of this book.
Please accept our apologies for any inconvenience this may cause.

Readers interested in further reading of Walt Whitman's poems
or his life might well start with *Walt Whitman: Complete Poetry and Collected Prose*
published 1982 by The Library of America or *Walt Whitman's America*
by David S. Reynolds, published 1995 by Alfred A. Knopf.
In addition *Walt Whitman: The Measure of His Song* published 1981
by Holy Cow Press contains essays by Alvaro Cardona-Hine and
Allen Ginsberg (a much expanded version of his essay in this volume).

Published in USA By Four Corners Editions
P.O. Box 20926
Mesa, Arizona 85215

THE OPEN ROAD
ISBN 0-9636501-4-9

1. Death-Literary Collection. 2. Whitman, Walt 1819-1892.
Title: The Open Road: Walt Whitman on Death and Dying
PN6071.D4064 1996
808.80354

Library of Congress Catalog Card Number 95-083495

0 9 8 7 6 5 4 3 2 1

Dedicated to our friend and neighbor, Joe Vest
1946-1994

Comrado, this is no book,
Who touches this touches a man,
(Is it night? are we here together alone?)
It is I you hold and who holds you,
I spring from the pages into your arms—decease calls me forth.

PREFACE

I come to this project with more than a little trepidation. Attempting to edit Walt Whitman is something like trying to edit a volcano. I feel, however, that it needs to be done. Not for Walt, not for poetry's sake, but because there are people who will profit greatly from reading these poems on death and dying–people who might otherwise never stumble across them.

I happened to come upon the first verses of *Song of the Open Road* at an entirely auspicious moment. Two weeks earlier, I had been diagnosed with full-blown AIDS. I was depressed, lonely and somewhat suicidal. Then I just happened to open an edition of *Leaves of Grass*. I was jolted from my complacent, self-absorbed depression into another world, a world full of real promise and music, by a beautiful and moving poem, and by the presence in the poem of a real and compassionate fellow traveler.

It was not some kind of "defiance" or "positive thinking" that moved me. Instead, it was the practical truthfulness of the poem. I could "take to the open road!" I was healthy, free, and the world was truly before me–the long brown path–leading wherever I would choose.

Ten years before, I had studied Whitman with Allen Ginsburg. I was attending a Buddhist seminary–a three month intensive sitting and study session in northern Wisconsin–where Allen was teaching a course on Buddhism and poetry. In the Buddhist tradition there are three paths that lead to enlightenment–the *hinayana*, the *mahayana* and the *vajrayana*. Allen had chosen various Western poets to represent the principles of the three *yanas*. For the *mahayana*, the path of openess, compassion and profundity, Allen chose Whitman.

I had loved *Leaves of Grass* since early adolescence. This class with Ginsberg completed the connection. Walt Whitman spoke for me in many ways–in terms of his expansiveness, his demand for justice, his sense that the universe was a mystery to be explored and enjoyed, not to be defined and limited.

One of the great moments of the class occured when Allen read *The Carol to Death* from *Memories of President Lincoln*. This poem celebrates death as an intricate part of life, a crowning moment, an epiphany. This joyful celebration leads to unexpected regions where the words "health," "wellness," and "healing" take on new meaning, redemptive meaning. It was this sense of "redemption" that inspired me in 1989 to begin the composition of an American *Requiem* based on Whitman's poetry on death and dying. It was the subsequent experience with performances of the *Requiem* that led to the idea for this collection.

Paul Joe Vest
1994

My brother, Joe Vest, asked me to finish this preface about one month before he died. He had been going blind for some time and was no longer capable of writing on the computer. I know this was supposed to be a gift, but I could not accept it. I had spent the last five years watching Joe and my other brother Jerry die from AIDS. Perhaps now, a year later and free of the torment of their loss and pain, I can say something to those who are left behind.

All the cliches are true, all of the descriptive passages about death are empty. While waiting for signs of the last breath the room always beckons for silence. When Joe died his friends had been sitting–meditating for two days. He became conscious the morning before his death with a gripping pain in his back. Joe told us to get a camera. This would make great footage. He felt like he was acting in a movie and he was dying and was doing a good job. He heard my voice as I was rubbbing his back, and he said "Oh Jan." He didn't speak again. I waited with him till 11 pm or so but needed to return to my wife and little boy at the hotel. I got the call at 3 am that said he had been dead about an hour.

The silence, the emptiness–forgive me Joe–the nothingness, is what's left. No smiles or laughter, no music, no dance–only tears, relief and loss. The love we had is all that remains. When I sing at church I hear his voice next to mine leading me to the correct note. When I play "Heart and Soul" with my niece, I see his hands instructing me so many years ago.

What a chance this has been, to see, to breathe, to love, to work. I say enjoy all of it, even as it passes.

Jan Vest
1995

I sit here with this collection of Walt Whitman's poems before me. Many I am reading for the first time. I think that each time I read them it will be as the first. I can imagine myself sitting with his big, burly form and his face fringed by that unruly white beard. His eyes are warm and mischevious beneath the brim of his Panama hat, like some outlaw Santa Claus. I can see that although he has passed through that gateway, in many ways we are still together. And so somehow I feel safer with my thoughts of death and dying.

Walt Whitman had the vision to see, in common appearances, the truth that we carry within. He seemed always to maintain, with ease, such freshness and innocence, even while exploring the realm of death. We get a taste of this in his poem, "A Clear Midnight:"

This is thy hour O Soul, thy free flight into the wordless,
Away from books, away from art, the day erased, the lesson done,
Thee fully emerging, silent, gazing, pondering the themes thou lovest best,
Night, sleep, death and the stars.

Whitman embraced everything in life as if it were his own dear lover. In his wanderings, he was able to savor whatever was put before him and he showed a bold appreciation for all that was given. Life was unquestionably precious, yet he did not fear death. He saw it as another opportunity, maybe the greatest opportunity to "move onward and outward." Whitman did not perceive death as an ending, or even a true beginning. And, on the night of the honeymoon between oneself and this lover Death, he saw us as challenged to bring forth all our knowledge, all our experience, all our humor, love, and fearlessness to move into that transforming embrace with utter dignity and in glory.

How could Whitman write so intimately of an experience he hadn't yet had? Oh, but he did have it. He recognized that we die frequently, in ways big and small, throughout our lives. There are the losses of loved ones through death or misunderstanding or pure growth. There are all the ways our perceptions and beliefs are continuously transforming, sometimes joyously, sometimes painfully but always changing. Night and day, success and failure, elation and exhaustion, growth and decay–in the company of these paradoxes we walk the chessboard of our experience. On a good day, we can appreciate these natural cycles as if we were strolling through a pristine grove, with sunlight and shadow paving our way.

I had the pleasure of knowing a man who chose to see the pattern of his own life and death in such a delightful way. His name was Joe Vest. He would come, almost daily to have lunch at the restaurant where I worked. Over time, I witnessed the decay of his health and body. But always, he wore a smile, a smile that grew increasingly more radiant even as his health continued to fail. I could actually see the life and light in Joe growing stronger every day, as if he couldn't wait to burst from his unreliable shell. Yet always he remained warm, laughing and joking with irrepressible humor about his situation. He brought comfort and ease to everyone he encountered, as if they were the ones ailing, and he, the healer. I think of Joe Vest this way, imagining him upon a great and wondrous adventure. Not because of my personal religious beliefs, but because that's how I see him feeling about himself. Joe truly came to embody the second verse of Whitman's "Song of the Open Road:"

> Henceforth, I ask not good-fortune, I myself am good fortune,
> Henceforth I whimper no more, postpone no more, need nothing,
> Done with indoor complaints, libraries, querulous criticisms,
> Strong and content I travel the open road.

And you who are about to undertake this journey, though it must ultimately be alone, perhaps you can gain some sense of comfort and fellowship as you share the visions of this high-hearted man, Walt Whitman. May you travel in peace.

Debra Floyd

WALT WHITMAN AND DEATH

> "…to die is different from what any
> one supposed, and luckier."
> Walt Whitman, Canto VI, *Song of Myself*

It is life, life only, that sees death and comments upon it, dreading the end of what it knows as itself and assuming, through a colossal lack of imagination, that what comes afterwards, if anything, is as blank as that which it assumes came before.

Consciousness thus plays a trick on itself; it doesn't see that here, for a short while, it has taken on the limitations of cohabiting–in a special, delicious but restrtictive covenant–with time and space. The covenant itself, this arrangement to be animal-angels, prohibits consciousness any knowledge of what came before, otherwise things wouldn't be what they are, we wouldn't be what we are, we wouldn't know this game of limitation, thirst, despair and opportunity.

It is only within that context that the human being thinks he knows what death is: an end. The end of the known. Hence our sorrow. And this unfair human being never dwells on the possibilities of the unknown. He shuns the poetic imagination. It takes a Walt Whitman to say that to die is different from what anyone supposed.

Different?

He is suggesting, and rightly so, that we know nothing about it. Even when we see a brother at death's door we know nothing. Oh, certainly, we see the weakness, the pain, or the grief, often the terror. But we don't see other things–the disentangling, the distancing of consciousness, the internal preparation that that person is unwittingly going through.

In an emergency, when we face imminent death, a distancing of consciousness takes place which is very peculiar and very comforting when rightly understood. A few years ago my wife and I were in a car accident, the vehicle we were in turned over. We both agreed afterwards that we had experienced a slowing down and a differing awareness of those moments when we were out of control and all matter surrounding us was most volatile and dangerous. Those lengthened moments just before the crash had an element of magic, of fairy inconsequence. We both understood–discussed it later–that our consciousness had distanced itself because it couldn't suffer. (Please remember: pain is different from suffering.)

So, what I believe this means is that consciousness, the soul, that which we truly are, is not interested in suffering, doesn't know how to be part of it. When pain threatens, it removes itself to an objective distance; we faint or see things differently. And if it can do that it must have a place where it goes–a womb, a cave of hibernation.

Perhaps Whitman is right when he says dying is different from what we suppose…

And luckier!

Luckier! How we wish it were so when we hear such words with our little everyday minds! Luckier! Is Whitman lying? Kidding himself? Poets and prophets don't say things they don't know. But how could we possibly spill over into that epiphanic mood so that it glows from within our entrails? So that we may be willing to leave the soft sunlight, the green earth, our loved one, the unfinished novel…

Luckier?

All that which gives us sustenance is the hand holding us aloft. If we pay attention to that hand, focus on it, we may begin to see that we are every part of its components, the infinite yet localized achievement of a cosmos that is then more than that hand. We are the effort it makes to see itself with pride and thanks. We are here to see, while we are alive, where we came from and where we go to, being luckier, closer to the Mother's breast, drinking of a milk that won't go sour.

Alvaro Cardona-Hine

THE POEMS & PHOTOGRAPHS

Song of the Open Road ❖ Wynn Bullock, "Child on Forest Road"

Of the Terrible Doubt of Appearances ❖ John Sexton, "Black Oak, Fallen Branch"

The City Dead House ❖ Frederick Sommer, "Max Ernst"

To Think of Time ❖ Aaron Siskind, "Peeling Paint"

Youth, Day, Old Age, and Night ❖ Ernst Haas, "Long Island, 1954"

When I Heard at the Close of Day ❖ Wynn Bullock, "Woman's Hands"

Whispers of Heavenly Death ❖ Wynn Bullock, "Sea Palms"

To You ❖ Ernst Haas, "Two Men, New York City, 1950"

On the Beach at Night Alone ❖ William Garnett, "Sand Dune #2, Death Valley"

Song of Myself ❖ Ian Berry, "Brothers Meeting at the Berlin Wall"

Full of Life Now ❖ Ernst Haas, "New Years Eve, Times Square, 1952"

Out of the Rolling Ocean the Crowd ❖ William Garnett, "Refelection on Rice Farm"

Of Him I Love Day and Night ❖ Henri Cartier-Bresson, "Couple in a Graveyard"

To One Shortly to Die ❖ Minor White, "Ivy, Portland, Oregon, 1964"

Joy, Shipmate, Joy! ❖ Ernst Haas, "The Ladies, London, 1951"

The Carol to Death ❖ William Garnett, "Sand Dune #1, Death Valley"

Portals & A Clear Midnight ❖ Eugene Smith, "Minamata"

O Living Always, Always Dying ❖ Linda Connor, "Baby feet"

The Last Invocation ❖ Linda Connor, "Embracing Trees"

So Long! ❖ Ernst Haas, "Truck, Utah, 1952"

Darest Thou Now O Soul ❖ William Garnett, "Snow Geese with Reflection"

SONG OF THE OPEN ROAD

Afoot and light-hearted I take to the open road,
Healthy, free, the world before me,
The long brown path before me leading wherever I choose.

Henceforth I ask not good fortune, I myself am good fortune,
Henceforth I whimper no more, postpone no more, need nothing,
Done with indoor complaints, libraries, querulous criticisms,
Strong and content I travel the open road.

The earth, that is sufficient,
I do not want the constellations any nearer,
I know they are very well where they are,
I know they suffice for those who belong to them.

(Still here I carry my old delicious burdens,
I carry them, men and women, I carry them with me wherever I go,
I swear it is impossible for me to get rid of them,
I am fill'd with them, and I will fill them in return.)…

The earth expanding right hand and left hand,
The picture alive, every part in its best light,
The music falling in where it is wanted, and stopping where it is not wanted,
The cheerful voice of the public road, the gay fresh sentiment of the road.

O highway I travel, do you say to me *Do not leave me?*
Do you say *Venture not–if you leave me you are lost?*
Do you say *I am already prepared, I am well beaten and undenied, adhere to me?*

O public road, I say back I am not afraid to leave you, yet I love you,
You express me better than I can express myself,
You shall be more to me than my poem.
I think heroic deeds were all conceiv'd in the open air,
    and all free poems also,

I think I could stop here myself and do miracles,
I think whatever I shall meet on the road I shall like,
    and whoever beholds me shall like me,
I think whoever I see must be happy....

From this hour I ordain myself loos'd of limits and imaginary lines,
Going where I list, my own master total and absolute,
Listening to others, considering well what they say,
Pausing, searching, receiving, contemplating,
Gently, but with undeniable will, divesting myself of the holds
    that would hold me.

I inhale great draughts of space,
The east and the west are mine, and the north and the south are mine.

I am larger, better than I thought
I did not know I held so much goodness.

All seems beautiful to me,
I can repeat over to men and women
You have done so much good to me I would do the same to you,
I will recruit for myself and you as I go,
I will scatter myself among men and women as I go,
I will toss a new gladness and roughness among them,
Whoever denies me it shall not trouble me,
Whoever accepts me he or she shall be blessed and shall bless me....

PLATE 1

Of the Terrible Doubt of Appearances

Of the terrible doubt of appearances,
Of the uncertainty after all, that we may be deluded,
That may-be reliance and hope are but speculations after all,
That may-be identity beyond the grave is a beautiful fable only,
May-be the things I perceive, the animals, plants, men, hills, shining
    and flowing waters,
The skies of day and night, colors, densities, forms, may-be
    these are (as doubtless they are) only apparitions, and the real
    something has yet to be known,
(How often they dart out of themselves as if to confound me and
    mock me!
How often I think neither I know, nor any man knows, aught of them,)
May-be seeming to be what they are (as doubtless they indeed
    but seem) as from my present point of view, and might prove
    (as of course they would) nought of what they appear, or
    nought anyhow, from entirely changed points of view;
To me these and the like of these are curiously answer'd by my
    lovers, my dear friends,
When he whom I love travels with me or sits a long while holding
    me by the hand,
When the subtle air, the impalpable, the sense that words and reason
    hold not, surround us and pervade us,
Then I am charged with untold and untellable wisdom, I am silent, I
    require nothing further,
I cannot answer the question of appearances or that of identity
    beyond the grave,
But I walk or sit indifferent, I am satisfied,
He ahold of my hand has completely satisfied me.

PLATE 2

The City Dead House

By the city dead-house by the gate,
As idly sauntering wending my way from the clangor,
I curious pause, for lo, an outcast form, a poor dead prostitute
    brought,
Her corpse they deposit unclaim'd, it lies on the damp brick
    pavement,
The divine woman, her body, I see the body, I look on it alone,
That house once full of passion and beauty, all else I notice not,
Nor stillness so cold, nor running water from faucet, nor odors
    morbific impress me,
But the house alone–that wondrous house–that delicate fair house–
    that ruin!
That immortal house more than all the rows of dwellings ever built!
Or white-domed capitol with majestic figure surmounted, or all the
    old high-spired cathedrals,
That little house alone more than them all–poor, desperate house!
Fair, fearful wreck–tenement of a soul–itself a soul,
Unclaim'd, avoided house–take one breath from my tremulous lips,
Take one tear dropt aside as I go for thought of you,
Dead house of love–house of madness and sin, crumbled, crush'd,
House of life, erewhile talking and laughing–but ah, poor house,
    dead even then,
Months, years, an echoing, garnish'd house–but dead, dead, dead.

PLATE 3

TO THINK OF TIME

To think of time–of all that retrospection,
To think of to-day, and the ages continued henceforward.

Have you guess'd you yourself would not continue
Have you dreaded these earth-beetles?
Have you fear'd the future would be nothing to you?

Is to-day nothing? is the beginningless past nothing?
If the future is nothing they are just as surely nothing.

To think that the sun rose in the east–that men and women were
    flexible, real, alive–that every thing was alive,
To think that you and I did not see, feel, think, nor bear our part,
To think that we are now here and bear our part....

Not a day passes, not a minute or second without an accouchement,
Not a day passes, not a minute or second without a corpse.

The dull nights go over and the dull days also,
The soreness of lying so much in bed goes over,
The physician after long putting off gives the silent and terrible
    look for an answer,
The children come hurried and weeping, and the brothers and sisters
    are sent for,
Medicines stand unused on the shelf, (the camphor-smell has long
    pervaded the rooms,)
The faithful hand of the living does not desert the hand of the dying,
The twitching lips press lightly on the forehead of the dying,
The breath ceases and the pulse of the heart ceases,
The corpse stretches on the bed and the living look upon it,
It is palpable as the living are palpable.

The living look upon the corpse with their eyesight,
But without eyesight lingers a different living and looks
     curiously on the corpse....

Do you suspect death? if I were to suspect death I should die now,
Do you think I could walk pleasantly and well-suited toward
     annihilation?

Pleasantly and well-suited I walk,
Whither I walk I cannot define, but I know it is good,
The whole universe indicated that it is good,
The past and the present indicate that it is good.

How beautiful and perfect are the animals!
How perfect the earth, and the minutest thing upon it!
What is called good is perfect, and what is called bad is just as perfect,
The vegetables and minerals are all perfect, and the imponderable
     fluids perfect;
Slowly and surely they have pass'd on to this, and slowly and surely
     they yet pass on....

I swear I think now that everything without exception has an
     eternal soul!
The trees have, rooted in the ground! the weeds of the sea have!
     the animals!

I swear I think there is nothing but immortality!
That the exquisite scheme is for it, and the nebulous float is for it,
     and the cohering is for it!
And all preparation is for it–and identity is for it–and life and
     materials are altogether for it!

PLATE 4

Youth, Day, Old Age, and Night

Youth, large, lusty, loving–youth full of grace, force, fascination,
Do you know that Old Age may come after you with equal grace,
    force, fascination?

Day full-blown and splendid–day of the immense sun, action,
    ambition, laughter,
The Night follows close with millions of suns, and sleep and
    restoring darkness.

PLATE 5

WHEN I HEARD AT THE CLOSE OF THE DAY

When I heard at the close of the day how my name had been
    receiv'd with plaudits in the capitol, still it was not a happy
    night for me that follow'd,
And else when I carous'd, or when my plans were accomplish'd, still
    I was not happy,
But the day when I rose at dawn from the bed of perfect health,
    refresh'd, singing, inhaling the ripe breath of autumn,
When I saw the full moon in the west grow pale and disappear in the
    morning light,
When I wander'd alone over the beach, and undressing bathed,
    laughing with the cool waters, and saw the sun rise,
And when I thought how my dear friend my lover was on his way
    coming, O then I was happy,
O then each breath tasted sweeter, and all that day my food
    nourish'd me more, and the beautiful day pass'd well,
And the next came with equal joy, and with the next at evening came
    my friend,
And that night while all was still I heard the waters roll slowly
    continually up the shores,
I heard the hissing rustle of the liquid and sands as directed to me
    whispering to congratulate me,
For the one I love most lay sleeping by me under the same cover
    in the cool night,
In the stillness in the autumn moonbeams his face was inclined
    toward me,
And his arm lay lightly around my breast–and that night I was
    happy.

PLATE 6

WHISPERS OF HEAVENLY DEATH

Whispers of heavenly death murmur'd I hear
Labial gossip of night, sibilant chorals,
Footsteps gently ascending, mystical breezes wafted soft and low,
Ripples of unseen rivers tides of a current flowing, forever flowing,
(Or is it the plashing of tears? the measureless waters
    of human tears?)

I see, just see skyward, great cloud-masses,
Mournfully slowly they roll, silently swelling and mixing,
With at times, a half-dimm'd sadden'd far-off star,
Appearing and disappearing.

(Some parturition rather, some solemn immortal birth;
On the frontiers to eyes impenetrable,
Some soul is passing over.)

PLATE 7

To You

Stranger, if you passing meet me and desire to speak to me,
    why should you not speak to me?
And why should I not speak to you?

PLATE 8

On the Beach at Night Alone

What can the future bring me more than I have?
Do you suppose I wish to enjoy life in other spheres?

I say distinctly I comprehend no better sphere than this earth,
I comprehend no better life than the life of my body.

I do not know what follows the death of my body,
But I know well that whatever it is, it is best for me,
And I know well that whatever is really Me shall live just
    as much as before.

I am not uneasy but I shall have good housing to myself,
But this is my first—how can I like the rest any better?
Here I grew up—the studs and rafters are grown parts of me.

I am not uneasy but I am to be beloved by young and old men,
    and to love them the same,
I suppose the pink nipples of the breasts of women with whom I
    shall sleep will touch the side of my face the same,
But this is the nipple of a breast of my mother, always near
    and always divine to me, her true child and son, whatever comes.

I suppose I am to be eligible to visit the stars, in my time,
I suppose I shall have myriads of new experiences—and that
    the experience of this earth will prove only one out of myriads;
But I believe my body and my Soul already indicate those
    experiences,
And I believe I shall find nothing in the stars more majestic and
    beautiful than I have already found on the earth,
And I believe I have this night a clew through the universes,
And I believe I have this night thought a thought of the clef
    of eternity.

PLATE 9

Song of Myself

I celebrate myself, and sing myself,
And what I assume you shall assume,
For every atom belonging to me as good belongs to you....

I have heard what the talkers were talking, the talk of the beginning
    and the end,
But I do not talk of the begining or the end.

There was never any more inception than there is now,
Nor any more youth or age than there is now,
And will never be any more perfection than there is now,
Nor any more of heaven or hell than there is now....

A child said *What is the grass* ? fetching it to me with full hands;
How could I answer the child? I do not know what it is any more
    than he.

I guess it must be the flag of my disposition, out of the hopeful
    green stuff woven.

Or I guess it is the handkerchief of the Lord,
A scented gift and remembrancer designedly dropt,
Bearing the owner's name someway in the corners, that we may see
    and remark, and say *Whose?*

Or I guess the grass is itself a child, the produced babe of the
    vegetation.

Or I guess it is a uniform hieroglyphic,
And it means, sprouting alike in broad zones and narrow zones,
Growing among black folks as among white,
Kanuck, Tuckahoe, Congressman, Cuff, I give them the same,
    receive them the same.

And now it seems to me the beautiful uncut hair of graves.

Tenderly will I use you curling grass,
It may be you transpire from the breasts of young men,
It may be if I had known them I would have loved them,
It may be you are from old people, or from offspring taken soon out
    of their mothers' laps,
And here you are the mothers' laps.

This grass is very dark to be from the white heads of old mothers,
Darker then the colorless beards of old men,
Dark to come from under the faint red roofs of mouths.

O I perceive after all so many uttering tongues,
And I perceive they do not come from the roofs of mouths
    for nothing.

I wish I could translate the hints about the dead young men
    and women,
And the hints about old men and mothers, and the offspring taken
    soon out of their laps.

What do you think has become of the young and old men?
And what do you think has become of the women and children?

They are alive and well somewhere,
The smallest sprout shows there is really no death,
And if ever there was it led to forward life, and does not wait at the
    end to arrest it,
And ceas'd the moment life appear'd.

All goes onward and outward, nothing collapses,
And to die is different from what any one supposed, and luckier....

PLATE 10

Full of Life Now

Full of life now, compact, visible,
I forty years old the eighty-third year of the States,
To one a century hence or any number of centuries hence,
To you yet unborn these, seeking you.

When you read these I that was visible am become invisible,
Now it is you, compact, visible, realizing my poems, seeking me,
Fancying how happy you were if I could be with you and become
    your comrade;
Be it as if I were with you. (Be not too certain but I am now
    with you.)

PLATE 11

Out of the Rolling Ocean the Crowd

Out of the rolling ocean the crowd came a drop gently to me,
Whispering *I love you, before long I die,*
I have travel'd a long way merely to look on you to touch you,
For I could not die till I once look'd on you,
For fear'd I might afterward lose you.

Now we have met, we have look'd, we are safe,
Return in peace to the ocean my love,
I too am part of the ocean my love, we are not so much separated,
Behold the great rondure, the cohesion of all, how perfect!
But as for me, for you, the irresistible sea is to separate us,
As for an hour carrying us diverse, yet cannot carry us diverse
    forever;
Be not impatient–a little space–know you I salute the air,
    the ocean and the land,
Every day at sundown for your dear sake my love.

PLATE 12

OF HIM I LOVE DAY AND NIGHT

Of him I love day and night I dream'd I heard he was dead,
And I dream'd I went where they had buried him I love, but he was
    not in that place,
And I dream'd I wander'd searching among burial-places to find him,
And I found that every place was a burial-place;
The houses full of life were equally full of death,
    (this house is now,)
The streets, the shipping, the places of amusement, the Chicago,
    Boston, Philadelphia, the Mannahatta, were as full of the dead as
    of the living,
And fuller, O vastly fuller of the dead than of the living;
And what I dream'd I will henceforth tell to every person and age,
And I stand henceforth bound to what I dream'd,
And now I am willing to disregard burial-places and dispense
    with them,
And if the memorials of the dead were put up indifferently
    everywhere, even in the room where I eat or sleep, I should
    be satisfied,
And if the corpse of any one I love, or if my own corpse, be duly
    render'd to powder and pour'd in the sea, I shall be satisfied,
Or if it be distributed to the winds I shall be satisfied.

PLATE 13

To One Shortly to Die

From all the rest I single out you, having a message for you,
You are to die—let others tell you what they please, I cannot
    prevaricate,
I am exact and merciless, but I love you—there is no escape for you.

Softly I lay my right hand upon you, you just feel it,
I do not argue, I bend my head close and half envelop it,
I sit quietly by, I remain faithful,
I am more than nurse, more than parent or neighbor,
I absolve you from all except yourself spiritual bodily, that is eternal,
    you yourself will surely escape,
The corpse you will leave will be but excrementitious.

The sun bursts through in unlooked for directions,
Strong thoughts fill you and confidence, you smile,
You forget you are sick, as I forget you are sick,
You do not see the medicines, you do not mind the weeping friends,
    I am with you,
I exclude others from you, there is nothing to be commiserated,
I do not commiserate, I congratulate you.

PLATE 14

JOY, SHIPMATE, JOY!

Joy, shipmate, joy!
(Pleas'd to my soul at death I cry,)
Our life is closed, our life begins,
The long, long anchorage we leave,
The ship is clear at last, she leaps!
She swiftly courses from the shore,
Joy, shipmate, joy.

PLATE 15

THE CAROL TO DEATH

Come lovely and soothing death,
Undulate round the world, serenely arriving, arriving,
In the day, in the night, to all, to each,
Sooner or later delicate death.

Prais'd be the fathomless universe,
For life and joy, and for objects and knowledge curious,
And for love, sweet love–but praise! praise! praise!
For the sure-enwinding arms of cool-enfolding death.

Dark mother always gliding near with swift feet,
Have none chanted for thee a chant of fullest welcome?
Then I chant it for thee, I glorify thee above all,
I bring thee a song that when thou must indeed come,
     come unfalteringly.

Approach strong deliveress,
When it is so, when thou hast taken them I joyously sing the dead,
Lost in the loving floating ocean of thee,
Laved in the food of thy bliss O death.

From me to thee glad serenades,
Dances for thee I propose saluting thee, adornments and feastings
     for thee,
And the sights of the open landscape and the high-spread sky
     are fitting,
And life and the fields, and the huge and thoughtful night.

The night in silence under many a star,
The ocean shore and the husky whispering wave whose voice
     I know,
And the soul turning to thee O vast and well-veil'd death,
And the body gratefully nestling close to thee.

Over the tree-tops I float thee a song,
Over the rising and sinking waves, over the myriad fields and the
     prairies wide,
Over the dense-pack'd cities all and the teeming wharves and ways,
I float this carol with joy, with joy to thee O death.

PLATE 16

PORTALS

What are those of the known but to ascend and enter the Unknown?
And what are those of life but for Death?

A CLEAR MIDNIGHT

This is thy hour O Soul, thy free flight into the wordless,
Away from books, away from art, the day erased, the lesson done,
Thee fully forth emerging, silent, gazing, pondering the themes thou
    lovest best,
Night, sleep, death and the stars.

PLATE 17

O LIVING ALWAYS, ALWAYS DYING

O living always, always dying!
O the burials of me past and present,
O me while I stride ahead, material, visible, imperious as ever;
O me, what I was for years, now dead, (I lament not, I am content:)
O to disengage myself from those corpses of me, which I turn and
    look at where I cast them,
To pass on, (O living! always living!) and leave the corpses behind.

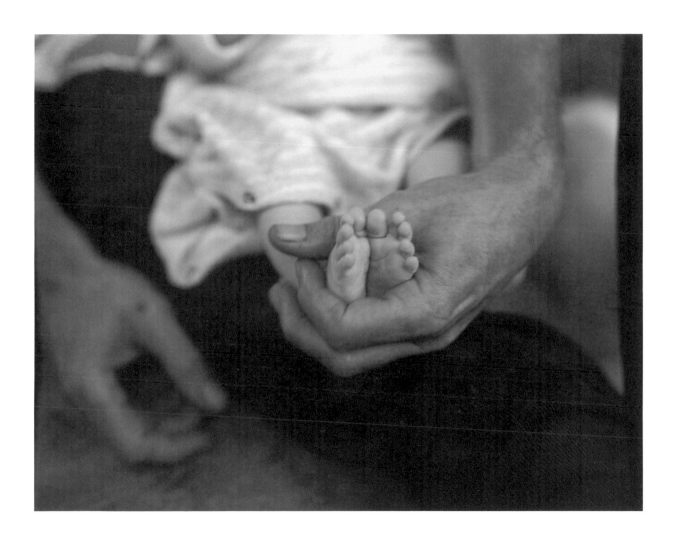

PLATE 18

THE LAST INVOCATION

At the last, tenderly,
From the walls of the powerful fortress'd house,
From the clasp of the knitted locks, from the keep of the
    well-closed doors,
Let me be wafted.

Let me glide noiselessly forth;
With the key of softness unlock the locks–with a whisper,
Set ope the doors O soul.

Tenderly–be not impatient,
(Strong is your hold O mortal flesh,
Strong is your hold O love.)

PLATE 19

So Long!

To conclude, I announce what comes after me.

I remember I said before my leaves sprang at all,
I would raise my voice jocund and strong with reference to
    consummations.

When America does what was promis'd,
When through these States walk a hundred millions of superb persons,
When the rest part away for superb persons and contribute to them,
When breeds of the most perfect mothers denote America,
Then to me and mine our due fruition.

I have press'd through in my own right,
I have sung the body and soul, war and peace have I sung,
    and the songs of life and death,
And the songs of birth, and shown that there are many births.

I have offer'd my style to every one, I have journey'd with
    confident step;
While my pleasure is yet at the full I whisper *So long*!
And take the young woman's hand and the young man's hand
    for the last time.

I announce natural persons to arise,
I announce justice triumphant,
I announce uncompromising liberty and equality,
I announce the justification of candor and the justification of pride.

I announce that the identity of these States is a single identity only,
I announce the Union more and more compact, indissoluble,

I announce splendors and majesties to make all the previous politics
    of the earth insignificant.

I announce adhesiveness, I say it shall be limitless, unloosen'd,
I say you shall yet find the friend you were looking for.

I announce a man or woman coming, perhaps you are the one,
    (So long!)
I announce the great individual, fluid as Nature, chaste, affectionate,
    compassionate, fully arm'd.

I announce a life that shall be copious, vehement, spiritual, bold,
I announce an end that shall lightly and joyfully meet its translation.

I announce myriads of youths, beautiful, gigantic, sweet-blooded,
I announce a race of splendid and savage old men.

O thicker and faster–*(So long!)*
O crowding too close upon me,
I foresee too much, it means more than I thought,
It appears to me I am dying.

Hasten throat and sound your last,
Salute me–salute the days once more. Peal the old cry once more....

What is there more, that I lag and pause and crouch extended with
    unshut mouth?
Is there a single final farewell?

My songs cease, I abandon them,
From behind the screen where I hid I advance personally solely
    to you.

Comrado, this is no book,
Who touches this touches a man,
(Is it night? are we here together alone?)
It is I you hold and who holds you,
I spring forth from the pages into your arms–decease calls me forth.

O how your fingers drowse me,
Your breath falls around me like dew, your pulse lulls the
    tympans of my ears,
I feel immerged from head to foot,
Delicious, enough.

Enough O deed impromptu and secret,
Enough O gliding present–enough O summ'd-up past.

Dear friend whoever you are take this kiss,
I give it especially to you, do not forget me,
I feel like one who has done work for the day to retire awhile,
I receive now again of my many translations, from my
    avataras ascending, while others doubtless await me,
An unknown sphere more real than I dream'd, more direct,
    darts awakening rays about me, *So long*!
Remember my words, I may again return,
I love you, I depart from materials,
I am as one disembodied, triumphant, dead.

PLATE 20

Darest Thou Now O Soul

Darest thou now O soul,
Walk out with me toward the unknown region,
Where neither ground is for the feet nor any path to follow?

No map there, nor guide,
Nor voice sounding, nor touch of human hand,
Nor face with blooming flesh, nor lips, nor eyes, are in that land.

I know it not O soul,
Nor dost thou, all is a blank before us,
All waits undream'd of in that region, that inaccessible land.

Till when the ties loosen,
All but the ties eternal, Time and Space,
Nor darkness, gravitation, sense, nor any bounds bounding us.

Then we burst forth, we float,
In Time and Space O soul, prepared for them,
Equal, equipt at last, (O joy! O fruit of all!) them to fulfill O soul.

PLATE 21

PHOTO CREDITS

ADDENDUM

POETIC VISION

by Jim Hughes

Make no mistake. Truth is as elusive for photographers as it is for poets. For generations, American school children have been led to believe that the camera never lies—that the images they see reproduced in newspapers and magazines, and now on their television screens and computer monitors, provide accurate witness to the events of the day. Yet most photographers learn early on that appearances deceive, that the real craft of photography is the art of illusion.

Minor White, whose allegorical vision is represented in this volume by a deceptively simple image of ivy caught seemingly in the act of climbing, once wrote that "...the state of mind of the photographer while creating is a blank...a very receptive state of mind, ready at an instant to grasp an image, yet with no image pre-formed...not unlike a sheet of film itself....The photographer projects himself into everything he sees, identifying himself with everything in order to know it and feel it better. To reach such a blank state of mind requires effort..."[1] It also requires, as White observed, a certain innocence, an ability "...to see as a child sees." With deep concentration, White believed, the photographer, while striving to record what a thing is, may actually reach the point where he or she depicts what else it might be.

White's stance certainly is not peculiar to the photographic arts. The poet Wallace Stevens, in his *Notes Toward a Supreme Fiction*, wrote:

You must become an ignorant man again
And see the sun again with an ignorant eye
And see it clearly in the idea of it. [2]

Is this not the crux of an idealized vision: to address the world not as it is, but as one wishes it to be? And would not an artist possessed by such a vision strive to show himself not as he is, but as he might be in this best of all possible worlds?

"I am large – I contain multitudes," Whitman wrote. "God is in the details," Stevens would reply nearly a century later.

"The fruition of beauty is no chance of hit or miss...it is as inevitable as life...it is as exact and plumb as gravitation," Whitman observed in his introduction to the 1855 edition of *Leaves of Grass*. "From the eyesight proceeds another eyesight and from the hearing proceeds another hearing and from the voice proceeds another voice eternally curious of the harmony of things with man....The art of art, the glory of expression and the sunshine of the light of letters is simplicity. Nothing is better than simplicity."[3]

Whitman addresses and celebrates death in its myriad forms. His poetry joins past, present and future: "...the consistence," as he wrote, "of what is to be from what has been and is."

Photography, on the other hand, its fragile moments sliced from the present and quickly consigned to our disparate pasts, has no such capacity to leap into the future. Photography's ability to speak well of death is limited to the coarsest of disciplines: the journalistic pursuit of war, pestilence, sadness, cruelty, man's inhumanity to man. But indignity is no fit subject for the Romantic vision; it must somehow be transformed. W. Eugene Smith, an artist hiding behind the mask of photojournalism, carried the requisite tools. Photographing Mr. Bunzo Hayashida in the throes of battle with an unseen enemy, Smith revealed his doomed subject with glancing stagelight, thus providing a gestural dignity that years of bedridden agony had denied. Within days, the helpless man was dead; an autopsy revealed the cause: Minamata Disease, mercury poisoning caused by industrial genocide. Mr. Hayashida, frozen in time by a kind of photographic immortality, lives on to teach us the lessons we never seem to learn.

If we accept the premise that from death comes life, then rebirth and transfiguration is the camera's cosmos. "I feel a responsibility towards the image as much as a writer feels for the word," wrote the photographer Ernst Haas, a transplanted Austrian who deepened his mastery of photography by studying poetry, and who brought an innate sense of harmony and beauty to a disharmonious world. "I am in search of images which reflect myself as much as they reflect the subject matter. I am not interested in shooting new things–I am interested to see things new."[4] His purpose in photography, Haas finally understood, has never been simply to document, but to transform as well. "Photography is a certain kind of loving," Haas once told a class of would-be photographers, and nowhere is this truth more evident than in the black-and-white images of people made early in his career. "A picture, really, you should be able to rest in it, sleep in it. And live in it. That for me is a picture."[5] For Ernst Haas, in fact, photography was poetry.

Walt Whitman, an American visionary from another time, would surely have understood this unwritten verse we call modern photography. As he wrote:

> Come said the Muse,
> Sing to me a song no poet yet has chanted.
> Sing me the universal.
> ...From imperfection's murkiest cloud,
> Darts always forth one ray of perfect light,
> One flash of heaven's glory.[6]

So in search of that perfect light, aerial photographer William Garnett looks down from the heavens to see symbolic equivalents of humanity in nature's patterns. John Sexton, a landscape photographer with his feet firmly on the earth, recognizes in the broken branches of a winter tree the end of life and its new beginning, repeated and repeated. Wynn Bullock stays close to home to make the familiar strange, which makes it familiar again, reminding us of ourselves. Linda Connor perceives love enveloped in love, animate and inanimate, wrapped and protected. Ian Berry has us find ourselves in others and others in ourselves. Aaron Siskind creates an infinite universe in a finite wall of peeling paint. Frederick Sommer looks right through the artist's temporal body to the toughness of man's spirit. Henri Cartier-Bresson shows us that in death, there are signs of life.

And we see that in these photographs there is poetry, pure and simple:

> 'Tis not for nothing, Death,
> I sound you out, and words of you, with daring tone–embodying you,
> In my new Democratic chants–keeping you for a close,
> For last impregnable retreat–a citadel and tower,
> For my last stand–my pealing, final cry."[7]

1 Nathan Lyons, Ed. *Photographers on Photography* (Englewood Cliffs, N.J.:Prentice-Hall, 1966, "Minor White," pp.165-66).
2 As referenced by Richard Ehrlich in his introduction to *Edward Weston:Leaves of Grass By Walt Whitman* (New York and London: Paddington Press, 1970), p. iv. This edition is a reprint of the original 1942 edition (limited to 1,500 copies) for which Edward Weston was commissioned to photograph Whitman's America.
3 Ibid., pp.xxii-xxiii.
4 Letter from Ernst Haas to the Magnum Photo Agency, 1960.
5 Class lecture, Maine Photographic Workshops, Rockport, ME, July 1981.
6 Whitman, from *Song of the Universal*.
7 Whitman, from *In Former Songs*.

Taking A Walk through Leaves of Grass

by Allen Ginsberg

There was a man, Walt Whitman, who lived in the nineteenth century, in America, who began to define his own person, who began to tell his own secrets, who outlined his own body, and made an outline of his own mind, so other people could see it. He was sort of the prophet of American democracy in the sense that he got to be known as the "good gray poet" when he got to be an old, old man because he was so honest and so truthful and at the same time so enormous-voiced and bombastic. As he said: "I sound my barbaric yawp over the roofs of the world," writing in New York City probably then, thinking of the skyline and roofs of Manhattan as it might have been in 1853 or so. He began announcing himself, and announcing person, with a big capital P, Person, self, or one's own nature, one's own original nature, what you really think when you're alone in bed, after everybody's gone from the party or when you're looking in the mirror, shaving, or when you're not shaving and you're looking in the mirror, looking at your long, white, aged beard, or if you're sitting on the toilet, or thinking to yourself, "What happened to life? What happened to Mommy?" or if you're just walking down the street, looking at people full of longing.

So he wrote a book called *Leaves of Grass*. And, in the final version of that book, the very first inscription was:

> One's-self I sing, a simple separate person,
> Yet utter the word Democratic, the word En-Masse.
> Of physiology from top to toe I sing,
> Not physiognomy alone nor brain alone is worthy for the Muse, I say the Form
>   complete is worthier far,
> The Female equally with the Male I sing;
> Of Life immense in passion, pulse and power, Cheerful, for freest action form'd
>   under the laws divine,
> The modern man I sing.

Well, that's kind of interesting. He starts with the female equally with the male, so he begins in the middle of the nineteenth century by talking about "women's lib": "The Female equally with the Male I sing." But he also says he's going to talk about the body, about physiology from top to toe, he's going to sing about the toes and the hair: modern man. This is on the very first page....

Democracy is also a key, which for Whitman means, in the long run, the love of comrades, that men will love men, women will love women, men will love women, women will love men, that there will be a spontaneous tenderness between them as the basis of democracy. He wants a democratic love, he wants an athletic love and he also wants a love in the imagination. He wants an expansiveness, he wants communication, he wants some kind of vow that everybody will cherish each other sacramentally. So he's going to make the first break-through–that's what he's saying. So he's got another little poem following that, "To You":

> Stranger, if you passing meet me and desire to speak to me, why should you
>   not speak to me?
> And why should I not speak to you?

Well, I don't know why not, except everybody's too scared to speak to strangers in the street, they might get hit for being thought a fairy or a nut talking in the subway or babbling to himself in the street. But Whitman was willing to talk to anybody, he said. Of course, he was living in a time when there was less fear....

Whitman was probably the first writer in America who was not ashamed of the fact that his thoughts were as big as the universe, or that they were equal to the universe, or that they fitted the universe. He wasn't ashamed of his mind or his body. So he wrote "Song of Myself," and it began tipping off where he was coming from and where he was going, saying that you, too, needn't be ashamed of your thoughts:

> I celebrate myself and sing myself,
> And what I assume you shall assume,
> For every atom belonging to me as good belongs to you.

> I loafe and invite my soul,
> I lean and loafe at my ease observing a spear of summer grass.

> My tongue, every atom of my blood, form'd from this soil, this air,
> Born here of parents born here from parents the same, and their parents the same,
> I, now thirty-seven years old in perfect health begin,
> Hoping to cease not till death.

Creeds and schools in abeyance,
Retiring back a while sufficed what they are, but never forgotten,
I harbor for good or bad, I permit to speak at every hazard,
Nature without check with original energy.

Wow! what a thing to do!…

So, what is he going to do now? What is he going to say next about where we all come from, where we are going?

I have heard what the talkers were talking, the talk of the beginning and the end,
But I do not talk of the beginning or the end.

There was never any more inception than there is now,
Nor any more youth or age than there is now,
And will never be any more perfection than there is now,
Nor any more of heaven or hell than there is now.

That's a great statement, very similar to what some of the Eastern, Oriental meditators, transcendentalists, or grounded Buddhists might say. Their notion is that everything is here already, wasn't born a billion years ago and slowly developed and isn't going to be dead a billion years from now and slowly undevelop, it's just here, like a flower in the air. There's never going to be any more hell than there is right now and never going to be any more understanding of heaven than there is right now in our own minds, with our own perception. So that means you can't postpone your acceptation and realization, you can't scream at your own eyes now, you've got to look out through your own eyes, as Whitman said, hear with your own ears, smell with your own nose, touch with your own touch, fingers, taste with your own tongue, and be satisfied….

…In the midst of "Song of Myself" he comes to a statement about the very nature of the human mind, his mind as he observed it in himself and when the mind is most open, most expanded, most realized, what relation is there between human beings and between man and nature. There are some little epiphanous moments showing, for one thing, his meditative view; for example in the fourth part of "Song of Myself" from "Trippers and askers surround me" down to "I witness and wait." Now that's a real classical viewpoint–the last person to announce that was John Keats, who said he had a little idea about what made Shakespeare great: "negative capability…."

In the Civil War, Whitman, following his instincts, followed the soldiers, went to

Washington, did volunteer work in hospitals, took care of dying men, was out on the battlefields as a nurse and saw Abe Lincoln on the streets numerous times. As Whitman was walking around on his own mission of mercy he wrote a lot of poems, like "A Sight in Camp in the Daybreak Gray and Dim"–this is a little snapshot, his same theme of human diversity in the midst of the degradation war:

> A sight in camp in the daybreak gray and dim,
> As from my tent I emerge so early sleepless,
> As slow I walk in the cool fresh air the path near by the hospital tent,
> Three forms I see on stretchers lying, brought out there untended lying,
> Over each the blanket spread, ample brownish woolen blanket,
> Gray and heavy blanket, folding, covering all.
>
> Curious I halt and silent stand,
> Then with light fingers I from the face of the nearest the first just lift the blanket;
> Who are you elderly man so gaunt and grim, with well-gray'd hair, and flesh all
>   sunken about the eyes?
> Who are you my dear comrade?
> Then to the second I step–and who are you my child and darling?
> Who are you sweet boy with cheeks yet blooming?
>
> Then to the third–a face nor child nor old, very calm, as of beautiful
>   yellow-white ivory;
> Young man I think I know you–I think this face is the face of the Christ himself,
> Dead and divine and brother of all, and here again he lies.....

Then in the midst of the tragedies of the war and his visions of death, there came the actual death of President Lincoln, and so his great elegy for Lincoln, "When Lilacs Last in the Dooryard Bloom'd" which most every kid in America knew back in the twenties and thirties, with its very beautiful description of the passing of Lincoln's coffin on the railroad through lanes and streets, through the cities and through the states and with processions, seas of silence, seas of faces and unbared heads, the coffin of Lincoln mourned, and in the middle of this poem a recognition of death in a way that had not been proposed in America before. Just as he had accepted the feelings of life, there was now the awareness of death that he had to tally finally.....

Then Whitman grew older, traveled, and extended his imagination to blue Ontario shore, and began to write about the declining of his own physical body in a series of poems called "Autumn Rivulets." He wrote about the compost ("The Compost"):

> Behold this compost! behold it well!
> Perhaps every mite has once form'd part of a sick person–yet behold!
> The grass of spring covers the prairies,
> The bean bursts noiselessly through the mould in the garden,
> The delicate spear of the onion pierces upward.

After the carol to death there is the realization of the recycling of body and soul, the inevitability of passage, transitoriness, of things entering the earth and emerging from the earth. He wrote poems about the city dead-house too. These were all autumn rivulets, including his "Outlines for a Tomb."

Incidentally, he arranged for his own tomb at that point, made up a little drawing which he took from the opening page of William Blake's last great prophetic book *Jerusalem*, of a man entering an open door with stone pillars on each side, stone floor, stone arch, a triangular arch on top with a great stone door opened, a man carrying a great globe of light. A consciousness entering into this dark, he can't see what's in it, like passing through with a big black hat. This tomb is now standing in Camden, New Jersey, exactly like Blake's image. He wrote little poems to his own tomb then and to the negative and began to consider the negative: how do you recompost the negative?….

…Most of the world is asleep, alas. His long poem "The Sleepers" was written earlier, before 1855, but he moved it into his poems of middle age. Death is coming a bit into his mind as he gets into his fifties and sixties. To him it appears that most of the people living in the world are the living dead or the sleepers….

"So long!" finally he says. "So Long" I think of as the last great poem of *Leaves of Grass*, a salutation and farewell and summary, conclusion, triumph, disillusion, giving up, taking it all on, giving it all over to you who are listening. "So Long!":

> To conclude, I announce what comes after me.

> I remember I said before my leaves sprang at all,
> I would raise my voice jocund and strong with references to consumations.

> When America does what is promis'd,
> When through these States walk a hundred millions of superb persons,

When the rest part away for superb persons and contribute to them,
When breeds of the most perfect mothers denote America,
Then to me and mine our due fruition.

I have press'd through in my own right,
I have sung the body and soul, war and peace have I sung, and the songs of life
    and death,
And the songs of birth and shown that there are many births.

I have offer'd my style to every one, I have journey'd with confident step;
While my pleasure is yet at the full I whisper *So Long*!
And take the young woman's hand and the young man's hand for the last time....

Finally he can with good conscience say farewell to his part, to his own fancy, to his own imagination to his own life's work, to his own life, in "Good-Bye My Fancy"…And that's counted as almost his last poem, but then he didn't die, he had to go on, poor fellow, thinking, allowing his executor to arrange *Old Age Echoes*, an appendix to *Leaves of Grass*, which ends with "A Thought of Columbus," a forward-looking poem about exploration, navigation, going into worlds unknown, unconquered, etc. "A Thought of Columbus" is not his most moving poem, or his greatest poem, but on the other hand is the last poem he wrote (December 1891) and contains maybe his last thoughts.

So, his life ended on a heroical historical note, congratulating the explorer, himself really, or the Columbus in himself, and the Columbus in all of us seeking outward in our spiritual journey looking not even for truth because it wasn't truth he was proposing, except the truth of the fact that we are here with our lusts and delights, our giving-up and our grabbings, growing into trouble and marriage and birth and growing into coffins and earth and unbirth. Good character, all in all, the kind of character that if a nation were composed of such liberal, large-minded gentlemen of the old school or young, large-bodied persons with free emotions and funny thoughts and tender looks, there might be a possibility of this nation and other nations surviving on the planet, but to survive, we'd have to take on some of that large magnanimity that Whitman yawped over the rooftops of the world.

ACKNOWLEDGEMENTS

So many friends have contributed in one way or another to making this book happen. We wish to thank Jan Vest, Mark Elliot, Joey Townsend, Francis Harwood, Kate Steichen, Steve Weinberg, Lance Grolla, Carolyn Pasternak, John Sharp, Carol Wilson, Cassandra Leoncini, Jerry Stroud, Ra Paulette, Sharon Alexandra, Dorothy Ebert, Katherine Corbett, Elizabeth Saliba, Emily Hunter, and Andy Jaicks.